TIM FLANNERY

EXPLORING THE INCREDIBLE WORLD IN THE TREES

WEIRD, WILD, AMAZING!

ART BY
SAM
CALDWELL

FOREST

FOR COLEBY AND DANIEL

First published in Australia in 2019 by Hardie Grant Egmont as
part of EXPLORE YOUR WORLD:Weird, Wild, Amazing!
Previously published in the US in 2020 as part of WEIRD, WILD, AMAZING!:
Exploring the Incredible World of Animals.

For information about permission to reproduce selections from this book, write to
Permissions, W. W. Norton & Company, Inc., 500 Fifth Avenue, New York, NY 10110

For information about special discounts for bulk purchases, please contact
W. W. Norton Special Sales at specialsales@wwnorton.com or 800-233-4830

Manufacturing by TransContinental

ISBN 978-1-324-01948-0 (pbk.)

W. W. Norton & Company, Inc., 500 Fifth Avenue, New York, N.Y. 10110
www.wwnorton.com

W. W. Norton & Company Ltd., 15 Carlisle Street, London W1D 3BS

0 9 8 7 6 5 4 3 2 1

TIM FLANNERY

EXPLORING THE INCREDIBLE WORLD IN THE TREES

WEIRD, WILD, AMAZING!

ART BY SAM CALDWELL

FOREST

Norton Young Readers

An Imprint of W. W. Norton & Company
Independent Publishers Since 1923

INTRODUCTION

I've been interested in animals and fossils for as long as I can remember. I grew up in the suburbs of Melbourne, Victoria, Australia, and there weren't a lot of opportunities near my home to see cool creatures. But when I was eight years old, I was walking on a sandbank at low tide and saw a strange rock. It had markings on it, and I suspected it was something special. I took it to the museum, where a man in a white coat brought me to a hall filled with gray steel cabinets. The man opened one, pulled out a drawer, and lifted out a rock identical to mine. "It's *Lovenia forbesi*," he told me, "the fossilized remains of an extinct sea urchin. They are quite common in the rocks near my home." It was, he thought, about 10 million years old. I was awestruck. Then he asked, "Are you interested in dinosaurs?"

could hardly speak. Learning about fossils led to a big breakthrough for me, and in the months and years that followed I would snorkel and scuba-dive in the bay near where I found that first fossilized sea urchin. I remember one winter afternoon, I spied a length of fossil whale jaw, nearly as long as me, lying on the bottom. Another day, I chanced upon the tooth of a megalodon shark lying in the shallows.

The man put the fossilized sea urchin back, closed the drawer, and opened another. "Hold out your hand," he said, as he placed an odd pointed rock on it. "This is the Cape Paterson Claw. It's a claw from the foot of a dinosaur, and it is the only dinosaur bone ever found in Victoria."

I held the Cape Paterson Claw! I was so excited that I

As I grew up, I went further and further afield, into the Australian desert and Great Barrier Reef, where I encountered water-holding frogs, red kangaroos, and magnificent coral. I became a mammalogist—someone who studies living mammals. For 20 years I was the curator of mammals at the Australian Museum in Sydney. I visited most of the islands between eastern Indonesia and Fiji, discovering new species of marsupials, rats, and bats. By the time I left the job I'd been on 26 expeditions into the islands north of Australia and discovered more than 30 new living mammal species.

I WAS MORE THAN INTERESTED. I WAS OBSESSED.

If you're interested in animals and nature, you can volunteer at a museum or on a dig, participate in a citizen science program like the Great Backyard Bird Count, or just start your own studies in a local tide pool or pond. If you decide to do a study by yourself, you need to take careful notes and send them to an expert in a museum or university to check them.

If you don't live near a beach, you can study nature in a local park or backyard. The soil and plants will be filled with living things, including birds and insects. But be sure to stay safe as you investigate!

If you're interested in fossils, keep your eyes on the rocks. Look out for curious shapes. And if you do find something, photograph it, or if it is small and portable, take it to your local museum. Most have services to help identify it.

When I was very young I often wished that I had a fun book that would tell me about the weirdest creatures on Earth. That's what I've tried to create here, for you. I hope that you find reading it to be a great adventure in itself, and that it leaves you wanting to see more of the wonderful and mysterious world around us.

Tim Flannery

EVOLUTION

Evolution is a word that describes how animals and plants change over generations. Each generation of living things is made up of individuals that differ a little from each other: some might be bigger, or more brightly colored, for example. And in nature, more animals are born (or germinate, if they're plants) than the environment can support. This means that the individuals that do best in their environment are most likely to survive. For example, if bigger, brighter animals or plants survive better, with each new generation the population will be made up of bigger, brighter individuals. Over many generations, the changes brought about by this "natural selection" can be so great that new species are created.

CLIMATE CHANGE

Earth's climate is changing because of pollution that humans are putting into the atmosphere. Greenhouse gases like carbon dioxide from burning coal, gas, and oil are causing the ground, oceans, and atmosphere to warm up. This might sound good if you live in a cold place, but many consequences of the warming are bad for living things. For example, warmer conditions mean that less water is available in some places, and creatures living in the warming oceans often have less food and oxygen. As seas rise and rainfall changes, and the atmosphere warms, entire habitats are disappearing, causing species to become threatened or even extinct.

SO SAD.

HABITATS

Habitats include places on land, in water, and even in the air. They are the places where animals live, and they vary greatly all across the world. Deserts are very dry habitats, tundras are very cold ones, while rainforests are very stable ones (with little temperature change, for example, between winter and summer). As animals and plants evolve, they become better adapted to their particular habitat. In the *Weird, Wild, Amazing!* books, habitats are grouped into four very broad categories: water, sky, forest, and desert/grasslands. Within each there are many different habitats—far too many to list.

FOSSILS

Fossils are the remains of plants and animals that lived in the past. The chances of you, or any living thing, becoming a fossil is very small. Maybe one in a billion! The first step toward a fossil being created happens when the remains of a plant or animal are buried in sediment like sand or mud. If the conditions are right, over thousands of years the sediment turns to rock, and the remains become "petrified" (which means turned to rock) or preserved in some other form, like an impression (such as a footprint).

COMMON NAMES v. SCIENTIFIC NAMES

Animals and plants have two kinds of names: a common name and a scientific name. The common name of a species is the name that you generally know them by, and these names can vary in different areas. For example, "wolf" is a common name in English, but wolves are called "lobo" in Spanish, and have many different names in other languages. But the scientific name never varies. This means that by using the scientific name, an English-speaking scientist and a Spanish-speaking scientist can understand each other.

Scientific names have two parts. For wolves, the scientific name is *Canis lupus*. The first part (*Canis*, in this case) is known as the genus name, and it is shared with close relatives. For example, the golden jackal's scientific name—*Canis aureus*—also begins with *Canis*. But the combination of genus and species name is unique. For wolves, the species name (*lupus*) means "wolf" in Latin.

EXTINCTION

Scientists use terms like "vulnerable," "threatened," and "endangered" to describe how likely an organism is to become extinct. Extinction occurs when the last individual of a species dies. If an animal is endangered, it means that very few individuals exist, and that they might soon become extinct. If an animal is threatened, it means that they are likely to become endangered in the future, while an animal being classed as vulnerable means that they are likely to become threatened.

ANIMAL TYPES

Animals and plants are classified according to their evolution. Animals, for example, can be divided into those with backbones (vertebrates) and those without (invertebrates). You can't always tell which group a plant or animal belongs to by just looking at them. Sometimes looks can be misleading! Falcons are related not to eagles or kites, which they resemble, but parrots. Parrots and falcons are classified in a group called "Austroaves," meaning "southern birds," because they originated in the southern hemisphere.

CONSERVATION

Conservation means taking care of nature and all of its plants and animals. Governments help by creating national parks, and fining litterbugs and polluters. Scientists play an important role in conservation by studying how we can help various species. You can be a conservationist in your own backyard: just plant a native tree that will become a home to the birds.

CONSERVE TO PRESERVE!

FOREST

TREE KANGAROOS

You might think you know what kangaroos are. They're large, furry animals that bounce through the Australian outback, right? You might also think there's no way a kangaroo could ever climb a tree . . . but you'd be wrong! Most kangaroos *would* look incredibly awkward if they tried to clamber up a tree, but not tree kangaroos. As you can guess by the name, these fuzzy creatures are related to kangaroos—but they live in the treetops. And, despite their large, lumpy bodies, they're remarkably agile up there! So tree kangaroos can climb trees—but how else are they different from the land-dwelling kind? Read on and you'll know everything in no time (everything about tree kangaroos, anyway—not *everything* everything. That would be a much bigger book).

A GROUP OF TREE KANGAROOS IS CALLED A MOB.

WHERE CAN I SEE A TREE KANGAROO?

Tree kangaroos live in the rainforests of northeastern Australia and New Guinea, and in the alpine meadows of Papua in eastern Indonesia.

BUILT-IN
RAINCOATS

Tree kangaroos have a special spiral-shaped patch of hair near their shoulders that helps rain flow off their furry coats instead of soaking through to their skin. This spiral of hair is in a slightly different place on each type of tree kangaroo, and the reason for that is pretty ingenious. Each type of tree kangaroo likes to snooze in a different position, and this built-in waterproofing system grows in the best possible place to keep rain off when they're sleeping in that pose.

NEW SKILLS

Tree kangaroos are descended from rock wallabies that learned how to climb trees. That's some pretty serious leveling-up!

FLANNERY FILE

I have been lucky enough to discover and name four species of tree kangaroos: **tenkile**, **dingiso**, **weimanke**, and **Seri's tree kangaroo**. The first three are native New Guinean names for tree kangaroos, but I named Seri's tree kangaroo after my best friend and companion in all my travels in New Guinea, Lester Seri. All of these tree kangaroos are found high in the mountains of New Guinea, in places so remote that other biologists hadn't found them. But the local people knew the animals well, and taught me a great deal about them.

Tree kangaroos are very hard to see in the forest. If they detect you, they will scramble around a tree trunk so that they are always on the opposite side of it from you, peeking around the trunk to make sure you aren't too close.

I have also cared for baby tree kangaroos whose mothers have been killed by dogs. They love to curl up with you at night, and to be carried around, making wonderful and affectionate companions.

CLIMATE CHANGE

Some tree kangaroos are found only in special rainforests or habitats growing near the summits of mountains where it's really cold. As the earth gets hotter, warmth-loving vegetation is growing ever higher on the mountains—so their habitat is shrinking. If we let climate change go on long enough, the habitats of these tree kangaroos will be pushed off the mountain summits and they will become extinct.

I'D RATHER BE NAPPiNG

Tree kangaroos can do death-defying leaps through the treetops, but they're actually pretty chill most of the time. They'd prefer to curl up on a branch, tuck their head into their folded arms, and do some heavy-duty snoozing.

HOW DO THEY GET AROUND?

Just like other types of kangaroos, tree kangaroos hop when they're on the ground. But they can also hop along high up in the treetops! Some types of tree kangaroo also walk along branches, one foot in front of the other. That's very odd behavior for a kangaroo, and they're the only kind that does it. If you're a tree kangaroo, one wrong step could send you hurtling to the forest floor far below. The stakes are quite literally *high*. Tree kangaroos aren't too worried, though, because they can jump huge distances without hurting themselves. Really, REALLY huge distances, like 65 feet straight down to the ground from up in the treetops. That's the length of 2½ buses! If you had technology like Batman you could give that a go, but otherwise jumping that kind of distance would do some serious damage to a human.

ONE OF THESE THINGS iS NOT LiKE THE OTHER...

Tree kangaroos look pretty weird. They're a type of kangaroo, but they certainly don't look much like the standard, feet-firmly-on-the-ground kind. Tree kangaroos don't even look like other tree kangaroos. Each different species has its own distinct style. Take these two, for example—they barely look related!

▶ **Dingiso tree kangaroos** have fuzzy black-and-white fur that makes them look like small pandas.

▶ **Goodfellow's tree kangaroos** are chestnut-colored with a yellow underbelly and paws. They also have two parallel yellow racing stripes running down their backs and bright blue eyes!

4

YOU CAN TELL A FRIEND BY THEIR SPOTS

Each **Matschie's tree kangaroo** has a different pattern on its face, and each **Goodfellow's tree kangaroo** has a different pattern on its tail. Scientists think that these intelligent species are much more social than marsupials usually are, and that they use the different patterns and colored markings to recognize friends or family at a distance. So, just how smart are they? Relative to the size of its body, Goodfellow's tree kangaroo has the largest brain of any marsupial!

A BELLY FULL OF WORMS

Each type of tree kangaroo has its own favorite food. Most also have stomach worms that help them digest their food. After tree kangaroos have eaten, the worms wait for the partially digested food to hit the stomach, where they have their own feast. The **dingiso tree kangaroo** has far more worms than any other species—about 250,000 worms in a single stomach! These wiry worms are as thick as hairpins and twice as long. Imagine having a bellyful of those wriggling around inside you!

WHAT'S IN A NAME?

Tree kangaroos don't look anything like hares, and yet their scientific name is *Dendrolagus*, which means "tree-hare." That's a pretty puzzling name! Maybe the 19th-century Dutch biologists who came across them in New Guinea tried eating them and thought they tasted like hares.

BABY TREE KANGAROOS

Tree kangaroos are smaller than a baked bean when they're born, and the first thing they have to do is climb into their mother's pouch to do some extra growing. They make this precarious climb up in the treetops, using just their front arms to cling to their mother's fur, as their back legs haven't fully developed at this stage. They definitely deserve a long rest in a cozy pouch after such a stressful start to their lives!

STAR-NOSED MOLES

Moles are cool, but star-nosed moles are *extra cool*. Like other moles, they spend a fair bit of time digging tunnels under the ground and gobbling down bugs. Unlike other moles, they also like to swim in rivers and marshy areas! If these furry little creatures could only ride a bike they could complete a triathlon. Their swimming abilities aren't the first thing people notice about star-nosed moles, though—they're too busy staring at the mass of fleshy tentacles growing out of their noses.

WHERE CAN I SEE A STAR-NOSED MOLE?

Star-nosed moles only live in North America, so if you happen to live there you're in luck!

A GROUP OF STAR-NOSED MOLES IS CALLED A COMPANY (OR A FORTRESS, LABOR, OR MOVEMENT).

UNDERWATER ADVENTURES

Star-nosed moles use their giant paws as spades to excavate dirt, but they also use them as hairy, claw-tipped flippers to glide through the water. That means they can hunt both underground and in the water—they're a double threat! Like humans, star-nosed moles blow bubbles out of their noses underwater. Unlike humans, they breathe those same bubbles of air back in! The bubbles trap smells inside them, so when the mole sucks them back in they get to breathe in any nearby scents, which helps them track down prey. It's just like sniffing, but underwater!

CLING-WRAP BABIES

Baby star-nosed moles are completely blind when they're born, and their eyesight doesn't improve much as they grow up. Their ears and nose tentacles are also sealed with a clear film, kind of like cling wrap, which they can't hear or smell through. So, as babies, they have to get by without three major senses. The film isn't only there for the first few hours, either—it stays for a couple of weeks! Luckily, their parents stick around to look after them for about a month, and then they can fend for themselves.

ARE THEY REALLY A TYPE OF MOLE?

Star-nosed moles started evolving in a different way from other moles about 30 million years ago. This explains why they do strange, un-mole-like things, like swim! Their closest relative is the desman, which is a small, water-loving mammal from Europe. Aside from burrowing into riverbanks, desmans don't dig at all— they come onto land to sleep, but spend the rest of their time in the water.

FASTEST EATER

Star-nosed moles mostly eat insects and other creepy-crawlies, such as earthworms. They also gobble down the odd fish. They're extraordinarily fast when they hunt, locating and scoffing insects in less than two-tenths of a second. This record speed earns it the title of world's fastest eater—not bad for an animal that can't even see its food!

ALL TEETH

Star-nosed moles have an astounding 44 teeth crammed into their slim mouths. Thankfully, they never need braces!

IS THAT AN OCTOPUS ON YOUR NOSE?

Star-nosed moles get their name from their bizarre noses, which are star-shaped and look like the bottom end of a wriggly pink octopus. Their noses have 22 fleshy tentacles, and they're incredibly sensitive—kind of like a superhero version of a human hand. Your hand has 17,000 nerve fibers to help you feel the things you touch. That sounds like a lot, but each star-nosed mole has a whopping 100,000 nerve fibers in its nose! The entire nose is only as big as the tip of your thumb, so they're packing all of that power into a really tiny package, too.

Star-nosed moles are almost completely blind, so they rely on their nose tentacles to get around and find food. They nod their heads constantly underground, bumping their tentacles against the earth to get a sense of what their surroundings look like. They can also feel things moving nearby by sensing vibrations in the ground—even tiny bugs can't sneak past!

00:30

THE AMAZING EXPANDING TAIL

In winter the tail of a star-nosed mole can grow to four times its usual size! They need to build up body mass to be ready to breed when spring arrives, so they store a lot of extra fat in their tails.

A MOLE FOR ALL SEASONS

The cold doesn't bother star-nosed moles. They can tunnel in snow just as well as they can dig through earth, and they keep on swimming even when the water starts to freeze. Their thick fur repels water and acts like a cozy jacket in the chilly winter months.

SMALL BUT STOCKY

A fully grown star-nosed mole only weighs about 2 ounces, which is about the same as a tennis ball. They grow to about 6 to 8 inches long, or about the length of a chocolate bar.

WHAT'S IN A NAME?

Male star-nosed moles are called "boars" and females are called "sows," just like pigs! Their babies aren't called "piglets," though—they're "pups," just to keep you on your toes. Their scientific name is *Condylura cristata*, which means "crested knob-tail." Their tails aren't exactly their most eye-catching feature, so the common name—star-nosed mole—suits them better.

CUTE!

SPIDERS

Sure, some spiders are incredibly venomous, and they can move startlingly fast on their many legs but, believe it or not, most spiders are not out to get you. Most of the terrifying things spiders do—like liquefying their prey or eating their boyfriends— don't relate to humans at all. And we get to admire the amazingly detailed patterns in their webs, and watch them do surprising things, like shaking their butts as they dance.

ARE YOU SCARED OF SPIDERS?

WHY?

A GROUP OF SPIDERS IS CALLED A CLUTTER OR A CLUSTER.

HAPPY FAMILIES

Starting a family can be pretty brutal for a spider. Some spiders don't even survive the mating process! Many female spiders, including the **black widow spider**, eat their partners after mating. Male spiders are often much smaller than females, so they don't stand much of a chance if their partner decides to make a meal out of them.

Australian **crab spider** mothers feed their babies with insects they have caught, but when winter arrives it becomes much harder to find food. Then, unable to nurture them further, she offers them one last meal—herself.

THAT'S DEDICATION!

DO ALL SPIDERS EAT MEAT?

All but one species of spider are predators. Most of them eat insects or other spiders, but a few are big enough to hunt lizards, rodents, and small birds. Spiders can only eat liquids, so how do they manage to eat these creatures? There are a few different ways. Most spiders either inject venom into their prey or vomit digestive fluids over them. Both of these things help break down the body of their prey until it can be slurped up. Some spiders spin silk around their food before they inject it with venom. That way their food turns into liquid in a tidy little container that they can eat out of easily—kind of like how you eat out of a lunchbox. Although spiders don't have teeth, some do have serrated pincers near their mouths that can be used to help grind up solid foods into mush.

So what about the one spider that isn't a predator? The *Bagheera kiplingi* from Central America mostly eats the leaf tips of the acacia trees that it lives in, sometimes snacking on a small amount of pollen, nectar, or ant larvae.

11

LORD OF THE DANCE

Some male spiders do elaborate dances to attract mates. One of the most incredible dancers is the **peacock spider**, a teeny-tiny spider with an amazingly colorful coat. These little guys scoot from side to side, stretching and shaking their legs. They often stick two legs straight up toward the sky, waving them up and down in a way that looks like they're clapping. The real showstoppers are their rear ends, though—these are the most colorful parts of the spider, kind of like the tail of a peacock, and they flip them up over their heads and wiggle them around as they dance.

CUTE!

ON THE HUNT

SOME SPIDERS DON'T BOTHER WITH BUILDING WEBS—THEY'VE COME UP WITH OTHER WAYS TO HUNT THEIR PREY.

- The **ogre-faced spider**, also known as the **net-casting spider**, doesn't use its silk to spin a web—it creates a net instead, which it holds stretched out in its legs to wrap around unsuspecting prey that walks past.

- The *Arkys* **spider** appears to attract male moths by mimicking the pheromones of female moths, then grabbing the males when they get close enough.

- **Trap-jaw spiders**, not to be confused with trapdoor spiders, don't build tunnels or webs—they rely on their wildly fast jaws to catch their prey. These super hunters sneak up behind their prey and snap their mouths shut over them with the speed of a rubber band being released.

- **Fen raft spiders** are relatively large spiders that live near bodies of water. They can walk across the water's surface by using the tiny hairs on their legs to spread their weight evenly. On top of their diet of insects and other spiders, these water-walkers also catch and eat tadpoles and fish!

- The **six-eyed sand spider** is a reclusive, crab-like spider that buries itself in the sand and ambushes prey that wanders too close. Sand grains adhere to it, providing a natural camouflage.

◀ FLANNERY FILE ▶

For more than 15 years I was the curator of mammals at the Australian Museum in Sydney. On one side of my office was the office of a snake expert and on the other side was the museum's spider expert. Accidents do happen in museums, and I've found myself, more than once, with a live snake lurking in my filing cabinet. Being surprised by a snake isn't exactly a pleasant experience, but the eccentric habits of the spider expert unnerved me even more. I'm not particularly afraid of spiders, but when I was dashing out of my office on an urgent errand and bumped into the spider expert, his hands full of deadly **funnel-web spiders**, I admit to feeling a little uncomfortable. He was a delightful fellow, but I dreaded visiting his office. Aquariums containing live spiders had been crammed into every corner, and the walkways between them were so narrow that the room was transformed into a den of oversized, hairy-legged creatures. Worst of all, he was so fond of his spiders that whenever I did come in he would reach into an aquarium and enthusiastically wave his latest spider in my face.

CLIMATE CHANGE

The impact of climate change on spiders is varied. Some will suffer population losses as their habitat shrinks, while other species' habitats will expand.

CAN SPIDERS FLY?

SPIDERS CAN'T FLY, BUT THEY CAN TRAVEL EXTRAORDINARILY LONG DISTANCES THROUGH THE AIR USING A TECHNIQUE CALLED "BALLOONING."

Some spiders can even travel across oceans! So how does ballooning work? Spiders climb something tall, such as a tree or bush, and then spin a number of long strands of web. They use these web strands to form a kind of sail that catches the breeze, lifts them up, and carries them through the air. If the breeze is gentle they might not get far, but if they're caught up in a powerful wind they could land anywhere! Ballooning isn't just some kind of extreme sport for daredevil spiders, though— when spiders need to escape flooding or other threats, ballooning can literally save their lives. Sometimes huge numbers of spiders balloon at once, leaving their landing spot covered in wisps of spider web.

SPIDER EVOLUTION

Spiders have been around for at least 380 million years, and they're still going strong! There are 38,000 species of spiders living in the world today, and perhaps as many again are waiting to be discovered and named.

WONDROUS WEBS

Each type of web-spinning spider has its own special way of building a web, and each web is designed to make it very tricky for prey to avoid or escape them.

▶ The **giant trapdoor spiders** of Southeast Asia and Australia make webs that look like silken tunnels. The spider lives inside the tunnel, setting up a number of delicate threads at the doorway to detect passing insects. The web jerks as the insects touch the tripwires, and when the spider feels the disturbance, it stalks out to pounce on its prey.

▶ The webs of the **orb-weaver spider** can be decorated with special, highly visible silk structures. They reflect ultraviolet light, which may help the spiders attract insects to the web.

▶ Some spiders make ladder webs more than 3 feet tall. These are very effective for catching moths, because moths are covered in loose scales that prevent them from sticking to regular webs. It is only when they lose most of these protective scales through tumbling down a ladder web that they are finally caught.

▶ Some webs are made of extremely fine silk. They are not sticky but instead work by entangling the legs of insects.

▶ A spider web's tensile strength, or ability to not break under tension, is similar to that of steel!

THE NOTORIOUS FUNNEL-WEB IS ONE OF THE WORLD'S MOST DANGEROUS CREATURES. IT LIVES IN EASTERN AUSTRALIA, AND IT HANGS OUT IN THE BUSH AND THE CITY.

UP CLOSE AND PERSONAL WITH . . .
A FUNNEL-WEB SPIDER

During the breeding season, males leave their burrows to find mates. They sometimes even enter houses, where they love to lurk in slightly damp places, such as towels casually dropped on bathroom floors. They can be very aggressive, so you really don't want to surprise one—if frightened, it's likely to bite.

Their fangs are strong enough to penetrate human fingernails, or even pierce the skull of a small mammal, and they bite over and over again to soak wounds with their venom. If you're bitten by a funnel-web you'll suffer excruciating pain, as well as convulsions, foaming saliva, nausea, blindness, and paralysis. If the bite's not treated it can take an adult 30 hours to die an agonizing death, but babies will die after an hour.

Like all spiders, funnel-webs don't actually want to waste their venom on humans. Why? Because venom takes time to produce, so if they waste it on a human they might not have enough left for things they can actually eat.

EEEK!

15

BEARS

Are bears adorable fluffy friends? Or are they terrifying hunters with claws and teeth sharp enough to tear unsuspecting prey limb from limb? Well, they're both! And they're plenty of other things, too—like dedicated parents, wrestling-mad siblings, living vacuum cleaners, tree-climbing enthusiasts, and long-distance swimmers, just to name a few. There are eight different species of bear, living in places as diverse as sweltering tropical forests and icy tundra, mountainous regions and lowland forests.

SOME SPECIES OF BEAR ARE SOLITARY, BUT GROUPS OF BEARS ARE OFTEN CALLED A SLOTH.

BIRD OR BEAR?

Sun bears and **spectacled bears** both spend a lot of time in trees, even sleeping up in the treetops. They're often too big to just sit on a branch, so they build the bear version of a nest—a platform made of sticks that they can curl up on.

CUTE!

HOW MUCH BIGGER THAN YOU ARE BEARS?

Polar bears are the biggest of all the bears. In fact, they're the biggest land-dwelling carnivores! Even though cubs start out weighing a measly pound, fully grown polar bears can eventually reach about 1,600 pounds. They can also grow to be nearly 8 feet tall, so they'd tower over adults—even the extra-tall ones, like basketball players!

COZY COATS

Polar bears have some of the thickest fur of all the bears. They even have fur on the soles of their extra-large feet, which makes padding around on the ice more comfortable. Their fur looks white, but it is actually clear. And each strand is hollow! These special features keep heat close to their bodies, and might even make it easier for sunlight to reach their skin so they can absorb vitamin D. Underneath all that fur their skin is black, and so are their tongues!

FRESH MOUNTAIN AIR

Pandas live in bamboo forests, usually quite high in the mountains. They can travel nearly 13,000 feet up into the mountains in search of food. **Spectacled bears** often live in particularly thick, lush jungles and are also great at living in high altitudes. They regularly climb over 13,000 feet into cloud forests.

STAY OFF MY LAWN!

- **Brown bears** often stand up on their hind legs and rub against trees to leave their scent on them. Leaving their scent can warn off other bears but can also help them to find a mate. They often rub so vigorously against the bark that it looks like they're dancing or scratching a particularly pesky itch.

- **Polar bears** also leave their scent for other bears to pick up on, and the way they do it is a bit gross. The sweat from their feet oozes onto the ice as they walk and leaves trails of smelly footprints wherever they go.

FLANNERY FILE

I once visited a bear reserve in Romania, where I hid in a very small camouflaged hut at dusk to watch a dozen bears feed on a dead sheep that had been left out for them. After night fell, I had to leave the hut and walk through the dark forest to get back to my car. My guide said that bears are more terrified of people than we are of them, but even though I knew we were safe it was still scary to walk through the bears' home at night!

RECORD-BREAKING NAPS

A lot of bears are up and about during the day, but others prefer to stay up all night.

- Despite their name, **sun bears** actually sleep during the day and are active by the light of the moon, not the sun!

- Bears often cozy up in some kind of den. Dens can be dug into the earth or made in caves and hollow trees. **Polar bears** dig theirs into the snow—it might still be chilly inside, but at least they're out of the bitingly cold wind.

- Not all bears hibernate, but plenty of them do—including **brown bears**. They settle into their dens and sleep through the winter, not even waking up to eat. All that time without a meal means they can lose half their body weight by the time spring arrives!

WHERE CAN I SEE A BEAR?

Bears are spread across the world—do any bears live near you?

- **Brown bears** are the most spread out, living in Asia, North America (where they're called "grizzlies"), and Europe.

- **Pandas** only live in China.

- **Sun bears** are found in Southeast Asia.

- **Sloth bears** live in South Asia.

- **Spectacled bears** are the only bears that live in South America.

- **American black bears** are only found in North America.

- **Asiatic black bears** live across Asia.

- **Polar bears** live only in the Arctic, in countries such as Canada, the United States, Greenland, Norway, and Russia.

CHAMPiON SWIMMERS

Bears can be great swimmers. Sometimes they get in the water to go after prey, but they often hang out in the water to cool themselves down, splashing and playing just for fun. **Polar bears** are particularly excellent at swimming. They have slightly webbed paws, which help them to paddle long distances, and the high percentage of fat on their bodies helps them stay afloat. Polar bears have been recorded swimming in the ocean hundreds of miles from land! They also hitch rides on floating ice to travel across bodies of water—some distances are too far for them to swim.

WHAT'S EVEN CUTER THAN A BEAR? A BABY BEAR! THEY'RE SMALL, THEY'RE FLUFFY, THEY'RE CUDDLY—WHAT'S NOT TO LOVE?

REAL LiVE TEDDY BEARS

▶ Bear cubs can weigh as little as a can of baked beans—sometimes even less!

▶ Cubs often play together, rolling around and tussling as they pretend to fight. These games aren't just for fun—they also help the cubs work out which of them are stronger and more dominant.

▶ **Panda** cubs are completely white when they're born.

▶ Sometimes **sun bears** stand up on their hind legs and cradle their cubs in their arms, just like a human mother.

▶ Baby bears are usually called "cubs," but can also be called "coy." Coy stands for "cub of

the year," and cubs can be called that when they're in their first year of life. Once they're a year or two old they are called "yearlings" instead.

▶ **Sloth bear** cubs sometimes hitch a ride on their mother's back—not many other bear mothers put up with being used as a method of transport!

WHAT DOES A BEAR EAT?

People often think of bears as terrifying carnivores, but not all bears hunt for their food—some prefer plants, and plenty of the meat-eaters are also content to munch on berries or a bit of honey.

- **Pandas** mostly eat bamboo, only taking a break from it occasionally to eat a rodent or bird. As they've evolved, one of their wrist bones has become more like a thumb, which makes picking bamboo easier for them. Pandas spend more time eating than you do sleeping—12 hours out of every 24! They eat an impressive 22 to 44 pounds of food each day.

- **Brown bears** love to gobble down moths—they can sometimes eat 40,000 of these winged creatures in a single day. They also love eating fish, especially salmon—they can grab them right out of the water, and often dive under the water to catch them instead of waiting on the bank.

- **Spectacled bears** mostly eat plants, including cacti!

- **Sun bears** use their long tongues to scoop termites out of their nests and honey out of beehives. They love honey so much that they're sometimes called "honey bears"!

- **Sloth bears** eat ants and termites. Their claws are over 2½ inches long, and help them break open nests. They blow away the excess dirt (to avoid eating it), and then they suck the bugs right into their mouths! They have a huge gap between their front teeth for the bugs to pass through, and flaps to seal their nostrils to give their mouths extra sucking power. They're a bit like furry vacuum cleaners!

CLIMATE CHANGE

Six of the eight species of bear are vulnerable or endangered, especially **pandas** and **polar bears**. As sea ice melts and gets thinner in the Arctic, polar bears find it increasingly hard to move around their habitat and find food.

SCRATCHING AN ITCH

It seems to be quite rare, but some bears use tools to make their lives easier—including picking up rocks to scratch themselves, even going after barnacle-covered ones for an extra-rough surface to really get in there.

TRYING A NEW DIET

Studies of fossilized bones have shown that Europe's **brown bears** were all carnivores before the Ice Age, and only started eating plants later on. Back then, a type of bear called a **cave bear** lived in Europe, and it only ate plants. After they became extinct 28,000 years ago, brown bears didn't have to compete with them for plant foods, so they started eating a lot more of them. When farmers arrived in Europe 10,000 years ago, they began to kill any bears that ate farm animals, so lots of meat-eating brown bears died. The vegetarian ones survived and bred, so today most of Europe's brown bears are largely vegetarian.

BIG APPETITES

Bears that hibernate during cold months, like **brown bears**, eat a lot of extra food as winter approaches. They go into a special state called "hyperphagia" that makes them drastically change their eating habits so that they can keep on eating for up to 20 hours at a time. That leaves just 4 hours each day for them to sleep! They can eat over 90 pounds of food each day during this period, which is like eating 40 large pizzas.

   Polar bears don't hibernate, but they still eat astoundingly huge meals when they can. They gorge so they have enough fat to keep them going when food is scarce—sometimes they can go months without a meal, and by eating big when food is available, polar bears can last a whopping eight months without food!

DOG OR BEAR?

Dogs and bears are related, and 30 million years ago they looked a whole lot more similar than they do now. In fact, some bear ancestors looked more like dogs, and some dog ancestors looked more like bears! It took millions of years for bears to begin to resemble the bears of today, and for dogs to evolve into their wolf-like shape.

HOW BIG IS A BEAR'S YARD?

Male **polar bears** have the biggest territory of any bear. They roam around on something like 110,000 or 140,000 square miles! Female polar bears make do with quite a bit less—more like 50,000 square miles.

BASILISKS

WHERE CAN I SEE A BASILISK?

Basilisks live in Central America and northern South America.

When you hear the word "basilisk," you're likely to think of a giant serpent with magical powers. So what do those mythical beasts have in common with these cool forest-dwelling lizards? Well, they're both reptiles for a start.

The ancient Greeks believed a basilisk was a monster made with parts of a rooster, snake, and lion that could turn people into stone just by looking at them! The scaly crests on the bodies of basilisk lizards do give them a distinctly rooster-like air. And although these lizards can't turn you to stone, they can certainly make you freeze in shock and amazement when you see them literally walk on water!

A GROUP OF LIZARDS IS OFTEN CALLED A LOUNGE, BUT BASILISKS DON'T HAVE THEIR OWN SPECIAL GROUP NAME.

AS BIG AS A DOG

The average length of a basilisk is between 28 and 30 inches, which is longer than the average golden retriever! **Green basilisks** can grow even bigger, stretching to almost 3 feet. A whopping two-thirds of a basilisk's length is just their tail.

TREE CHANGE

Some basilisk species spend most of their time on the ground, whereas others prefer to lurk up in the treetops of their forest homes. They have sharp claws to help them grip onto bark, and they regularly climb more than 20 feet up into the trees.

One thing that all basilisks have in common is the desire to live near water, generally the banks of rivers. They rely on this watery back door as a method of escape if things get too dangerous on land!

TAKING A DIP

Although they can stay dry by running on the water's surface, basilisks are also great at swimming. They don't swim only for fun—they can hold their breath and hide under the surface for up to half an hour, which is a handy way of escaping land predators.

MIRACLE WORKERS

Basilisks can walk on water—which is how they earned the nickname "Jesus lizard." They usually walk on water to escape predators on land. It isn't a graceful walk—they stand upright and rotate their back legs rapidly, kind of like they're pedaling an invisible bike. Their arms stick out stiffly on either side and their whole body sways as they gallop along, head bobbing from right to left. Here are the mechanics:

▶ Their back feet are special—they're HUGE, which allows them to spread their weight over a wider surface (a bit like snowshoes). And their feet have extra flaps of skin on them; as they slam their feet down on the water, these flaps trap air bubbles that help keep them afloat.

▶ They need to move FAST to stop themselves from sinking—if they slow down, the air bubbles won't form and their feet will start to become submerged.

▶ Their tails play an important part, helping them to stay balanced and change direction.

▶ Basilisks usually start with a run-up on land, but they can also leap straight down from the trees onto the water below.

▶ They can run for a stretch of 30 to 70 feet across the water, and the youngest, lightest specimens are the fastest.

23

CHAMELEONS

If someone calls you a chameleon, they mean you're good at changing yourself in some way to suit a particular environment. But no matter how good humans are at switching things up to fit in, they can't truly compare to actual chameleons! These lizards are seriously incredible at blending in, but they're just as likely to be bright and flashy so they stand out. And if you think their skin is cool, wait until you hear about what's underneath it . . .

CAT OR LIZARD?

"Chameleon" is Greek for "on-the-ground lion"!

POINTLESS POISON

Some chameleons have venom glands, but they are atrophied and don't produce enough venom to do any damage to anything.

WHERE CAN I SEE A CHAMELEON?

About half of all chameleon species live in Madagascar, with the others sprinkled across small nearby islands and through Kenya, Tanzania, and other African countries. They also live in India, Sri Lanka, Spain, Portugal, and parts of the Middle East.

MOVING OVERSEAS

The oldest chameleon fossils are 60 million years old, and were discovered in China. However, there are no living chameleons left there today.

OPTIONAL EGGSHELLS

▶ When it comes to starting families, males with the brightest colors are at an advantage—female chameleons are more likely to mate with them.

▶ For one particular chameleon, **Labord's chameleon**, there's no time to waste when it comes to having babies—this particular species only lives for a total of three months.

▶ Some chameleons, like **Jackson's chameleon**, have live babies, like humans do. Other species lay eggs. Imagine if some of your cousins hatched out of an egg!

▶ Chameleons can lay up to 100 eggs at a time. Up to 30 live babies can be born at a time, but it's often fewer.

▶ Chameleon eggs are usually buried in burrows that the mothers dig into dirt or rotting wood.

▶ Parents don't look after their babies—they don't even wait around to see them hatch! To be fair, eggs usually don't hatch for about a year, and the eggs of some species can take a whopping two years to incubate, so they'd be waiting a long time.

ARE THEY MAGIC?

Sometimes color changes are gradual, but they can also happen very rapidly—in minutes, or even seconds. Chameleons don't use magic to change color, but they do use crystals! They have different layers of skin, and each one does its own special thing.

▶ The top layer of skin is covered with cells that are filled with pigment. These cells expand and contract to make the chameleon darker or lighter— they only alter the shade, not the color.

▶ The lower layers of skin have cells called "iridophores," which are filled with small crystals. They change shape in reaction to the chameleon's mood. They reflect light differently, depending on how contracted or expanded they are, which is what changes the color of the skin. The shape of the cells affects the color of the skin, and so does the amount of space between each crystal-filled cell. The cells move further apart when the chameleon is excited and closer together when it's relaxed.

▶ There is a layer of skin even further down that only reflects a certain kind of light—infrared light. Scientists think this might help chameleons regulate their temperature.

25

KEEPING AN EYE ON THINGS

Chameleon eyes are extraordinarily powerful. They have 360-degree vision, and each eye can point in completely different directions at the same time. They also work like camera lenses—they have a built-in function for zooming in to get a closer look at something in the distance.

HOW **BIG** IS A CHAMELEON?

The smallest chameleon is the **Brookesia micra**, which is often less than 1 inch long when fully grown—so they're small enough to sit on your little finger! The largest is the **Parson's chameleon**, which can grow to up to 27 inches. Even your entire arm isn't long enough for them to sit on!

LiZARD OR LEAF?

Some chameleons don't need to change color to blend in—their natural shape, size, and color already make them nearly invisible. **Decary's leaf chameleons** look just like brown leaves!

FLANNERY FILE

I love chameleons and have often seen them on my travels in Africa. Once I was riding a horse in Botswana and I saw a giant **ground chameleon**. It was gray and standing on a sand dune, pretending to be a dead stick. It was completely still, with its tail sticking straight up in the air, and I almost got off my horse to take a closer look, but was very glad I didn't when I saw the paw prints of a huge lion next to the chameleon! The prints were so fresh that sand was still dribbling into them, so I turned around and galloped off as fast as I could.

ALL THE COLORS OF THE RAINBOW?

Chameleons can't just pick any color to change into—each of the 200 species has a specific range of color options, so the idea that they can change color to blend into any background is a myth.

▶ When they're just chilling out, most chameleons are shades of brown and green—the colors that are more likely to blend in with their forest environments.

▶ It's not just their colors that can change—patterns, such as spots or stripes, can also appear on a chameleon's skin.

▶ Males are generally more likely to change color, and often have a wider range of colors than females. Sometimes males and females of the same species are very different colors.

FLASHY AND FiERCE

Changing color can help chameleons blend into their environment, but that isn't the main reason they do it. Color shifts also help chameleons communicate with each other. Their color shifts can say a lot about how they're feeling—if they're angry, or want to mate, or are trying to send a warning, for instance.

▶ Males are territorial and use their brightest displays to stand out and intimidate other males. Sometimes they turn bright red—a warning sign in most languages. In a standoff, one male will eventually concede defeat by returning to a duller color. Males can get physical if color-changing doesn't scare off another male. They will puff up, hiss, snap, headbutt, and charge each other, grappling until one backs down.

▶ Males get an extra-flashy set of colors, including various combinations of turquoise, blue, green, orange, yellow, and red, when they want to attract a mate. Females can communicate that they don't want to mate by changing color, often becoming darker with bright splashes of color. That can be particularly helpful when they're already pregnant.

▶ Sometimes male chameleons (especially smaller, younger ones) change color to look like females so other males won't become territorial and try to fight them.

UP IN THE TREES Ⓥ DOWN IN THE DIRT

▶ A lot of chameleon species spend the majority of their time in trees, using their prehensile tails to wrap around branches as they climb—a bit like a much longer, more flexible limb. When they're not using their tails they often curl them up into a tight spiral.

▶ A limited number of species spend more time on the ground, such as the **horned leaf chameleon** and **Gorongosa pygmy chameleon**. Some of these ground-dwellers climb up into trees for extra protection when sleeping, but otherwise they use camouflage to blend into leaf litter on the forest floor. Some of these species don't even have prehensile tails—in fact, theirs can be quite short and stumpy.

▶ Chameleons have very flexible ankles and wrists, plus specially shaped feet that help them grip onto branches and bark. They look like they only have two fat toes on each foot, but each toe is actually several smaller ones fused together into one mega toe. That's why what looks like one toe can have multiple claws on it!

27

SKUNKS

The smell skunks let off is called "musk"—but not the good kind. Their scientific name, Mephitidae, comes from the Latin name for an ancient goddess of noxious gases, like the stinky ones that waft out of swamps and volcanoes. So that gives you an idea of what they smell like! There's more to these animals than their smell, though. They can be strikingly beautiful and athletic.

WHAT IS A GROUP OF SKUNKS CALLED?

A group of skunks is called a "surfeit," which is a word that means an excessive amount of something. For some people, especially those with sensitive noses, even one skunk is too many, so a group of any size would certainly seem like a surfeit!

WHEN YOU THINK OF SKUNKS, YOU THINK STINK.

WHERE CAN I SEE A SKUNK?

Skunks live in South and North America. **Stink badgers**, despite their name, are a type of skunk. They live in the Philippines and Indonesia.

WHAT'S ON THE MENU?

Skunks use their claws to rifle and dig through leaf litter to uncover food, which often consists of insects. But they're not fussy. They also eat things like fruit, eggs, fish, reptiles, larvae, and small mammals such as mice or moles. Sometimes they even go after snakes!

Skunks are resistant to the venom of some kinds of snakes, so they have less reason to fear slithery predators than many other small, furry animals.

SUPER MOMS

Female skunks are very independent, preferring to raise their babies alone. They make this clear to their partners not long after mating—sometimes even chasing away the males! After mating, female skunks don't always become pregnant right away. The **western spotted skunk** often waits up to 150 days after mating to start growing babies inside her womb. The father is definitely long gone by then!

Skunk babies, also known as "kits," are completely blind when they're born. Their eyes are sealed shut for the first three weeks of their lives, so they count on their moms to feed and take care of them.

WHY THE STRIPES?

It is thought that the striped pattern on many skunks is connected to their defensive abilities. The white lines on their fur direct predators' eyes toward the source of their stink—their butts!

HOW BIG IS A SKUNK?

The **hog-nosed skunk** is one of the largest skunks, sometimes stretching over 2.5 feet—similar to the length of a labrador. A fair bit of their length comes from their tail, though, so even though they look big, they usually only weigh as much as 10 pounds.

That's barely half the weight of a wiener dog!

On the other end of the scale is the **pygmy spotted skunk**, which is often under 8 inches long. With its tail curled around it, you could hold one of these little critters in your hand!

FLANNERY FILE

A creature remarkably similar to skunks inhabits northern Australia and New Guinea. These **striped possums** (also sometimes known as skunk possums) are small, cat-sized marsupials strikingly striped in black and white. One type has a massively bushy tail like some skunks, and some New Guineans wear its black-and-silver tail as a false beard! The four known species of striped possum all live in the rainforest, and, as I discovered when studying them in New Guinea, they have a very strong smell that really is skunk-like, though not nearly as awful. You can locate where they have been feeding or denning in hollow logs or tree hollows by their smell. Luckily, they cannot spray their odor. But if you handle one, the stench can stick to your hands for days!

WHICH SKUNK IS WHICH?

Not all skunks have stripes! There are five main types of skunk, and the white on their fur can appear in all sorts of patterns, or not at all—some are black all over.

▶ The **striped skunk** has two long stripes down its back, while the **spotted skunk** is covered in swirls and splotches of white.

▶ **Hog-nosed skunks** can have stripes, but sometimes have one huge swath of white down their backs instead. They also have a particularly memorable nose—completely bare of fur and quite large, kind of like the snout on a pig or a hog.

▶ **Stink badgers** can have lots of different kinds of white marks, but often don't have any white markings at all. They also have much shorter tails than other skunk species.

▶ **Hooded skunks** have extra-long tails and super-soft fur, which is particularly long around the back of their head and neck. Sometimes they have small amounts of white on their black fur, other times they have a long patch of white from the top of their head to the tip of their tail.

HOW DO YOU GET RID OF SKUNK SMELLS?

Skunk musk can't be washed off easily—even taking a shower won't get rid of it. There are all sorts of strange things people use to try to get rid of the stink, including vanilla extract, tomato juice, and apple cider vinegar. None of those things are a match for skunk musk, though. One of the most popular remedies uses baking soda, dish soap, and hydrogen peroxide, but hopefully you never have to test it out!

A HOLE TO CALL HOME

Skunks spend most of their time on the ground, with the exception of **spotted skunks**—they can climb trees so well that they're sometimes called "tree skunks." Skunks often live in burrows underground or cozy up in hollow logs and crevices in rocks.

STINK

- When skunks are feeling threatened by predators, they spray an oily substance out of two nipple-like areas just inside their butthole.

- Skunk stink takes days to wear off, but it isn't toxic. The point is to scare off predators, not kill them!

- If you get sprayed, you'll probably feel a burning sensation, plus you can temporarily lose your vision and have trouble breathing. It can also make you puke!

- Skunks can shoot their stink as far as 33 feet, but the closer the target, the more accurate their aim is.

- Skunks can spray out either a cloud or a concentrated jet of stink—a bit like adjusting the nozzle on a spray-bottle. The jet is usually used when they are close to an attacker and can aim right at their face. The cloud isn't quite as effective, but it's useful for covering a large area when the skunk can't aim as well, such as when it is running away!

- Skunk spray and onions contain some of the same type of chemicals, which helps explain why both can make your eyes water.

MOST PEOPLE KNOW THAT SKUNKS SMELL TERRIBLE. BUT WHY DO THEY HAVE SUCH A PECULIAR STENCH, AND WHERE DOES IT COME FROM?

- Skunks often try to frighten off attackers using other means before resorting to using their smelly spray. They make hissing or snarling sounds, stamp their front feet, arch their backs, and raise their tails in the air. Some even charge their attackers. **Hog-nosed skunks** sometimes stand all the way up on their hind legs before crashing back down onto all fours.

- Some **spotted skunks**, like the **eastern spotted skunk**, do a handstand before they release their spray. They fan out their tails above them to look bigger, keeping an eye on their attacker to see if their intimidation tactic is working.

Sometimes they even charge at their attacker while upside down, moving quickly on their hands like some sort of stinky acrobat.

- Some people can't smell skunk musk—those people are rare, but lucky!

31

SLOTHS

There are two main kinds of sloth: the **two-toed** and the **three-toed**. It sounds like the difference between them is obvious—they have different numbers of toes, right? Correct! But that's not all. These sloths are actually very distant relatives, not two members of the same genus! That doesn't stop them from having heaps in common—they're slow, they like munching leaves, and they're prone to napping. Most people know those things about sloths already, but do you know what happens when you put one in water? Or what's special about the bones in their fingers, or their poo?

A GROUP OF SLOTHS IS SOMETIMES CALLED A BED.

SLOW MOVERS

Sloths are the slowest mammals in the world, without exception. Their climbing speed is usually only about 6 to 8 feet per minute at the most—sometimes even slower.

WHERE CAN I SEE A SLOTH?

Sloths live in South and Central America.

LIFE IN THE
TREES

Sloths don't bother leaving their trees to mate—everything happens up in the treetops, from finding a suitable partner to giving birth. When they're ready to start a family, female sloths have a special way of announcing it. They yell! Their loud call can sometimes sound like a whistle or a scream. Sloths have one baby at a time and raise it high up in the trees. Since sloths don't have pouches, each tiny baby has to hold on tight to its mother's hairy tummy to avoid falling to the ground.

DEATH GRIPS

Sloths are famous for being lazy. They sleep for about nine hours a day, and they move very slowly (if at all) the rest of the time. But how can they possibly rest easy when they're way up high in the rainforest canopy? Sometimes they find a cozy fork to curl up in, but more often than not they fall asleep hanging upside down from a branch. They have to rely on their arms and claws to stop them from falling, and luckily for them both are incredibly strong. So strong, in fact, that even when sloths die, they rarely fall out of the trees. Their arms keep on clinging to the branch they were dangling from when they took their last breath.

HOW BIG IS A SLOTH?

Two-toed sloths are sometimes a little bigger than their **three-toed** counterparts, but both types usually weigh somewhere between 8 and 18 pounds—about the same as a small pug. They grow up to 27 inches tall, but their limbs are so long that they often look a lot larger! The **pygmy three-toed sloth** is the smallest sloth. It only lives on one island in Panama called Escudo de Veraguas, and can be as short as 19 inches. It weighs as little as 5.5 pounds, which is similar to a chihuahua.

CLAW OR SWORD?

Why are sloths so slow? It's to keep them safe from predators! They don't have many ways to protect themselves, so if they can avoid being noticed by a predator in the first place, they won't have to worry about outrunning them or fighting them off. Just about the only method of defense sloths do have is their claws, which can be a whopping 4 inches long. Sloth claws aren't anything like your fingernails—they're actually part of the sloth's finger bones covered in a fingernail-like sheath.

TEARS OF . . .
BLOOD

Some **three-toed sloths** can occasionally be seen with red liquid leaking from their eyes. That sounds bad, right? But it's actually perfectly normal eye goop—a bit like the crusty gunk you get in the corners of your eyes in the morning. The reason it's red is that these sloths eat a particular kind of red-tinged leaf, and it dyes their eye goo.

DOWNSIZING

Ancient sloths were hugely different from the ones you can see today—emphasis on the HUGE. They weighed up to 7.7 tons, which is more than some species of elephant!

SWIMMING LAPS

You wouldn't expect sloths to be good at swimming, but they are! One extinct kind of **giant sloth** even swam in the Pacific Ocean off South America and ate seaweed.

Modern-day sloths often drop straight down from trees into water, paddling around and using their long front arms to cut through the water. They're actually three times faster in the water than they are on land! But in classic sloth fashion, they don't swim quickly all that often—they like to lie back and let the water hold them up. Being quite light makes floating easier for them, and the gas in their stomachs created by the digestion process also helps them stay afloat.

SUPER STOMACHS

KEEPING COZY

Three-toed sloths often seek out the sun, climbing high up in the trees to sunbathe. It's important for them to stay warm, because sloths can't shiver to warm up—it uses too much energy!

Sloths are leaf connoisseurs—they eat HEAPS of them. **Two-toed sloths** eat quite a few different things aside from leaves, including insects, fruit, and even lizards. **Three-toed sloths** are much fussier by comparison—they eat leaves from just a few species of trees. Digesting all those leaves isn't easy, but

luckily sloths have stomachs specially made to do just that. They are made up of four different parts and are packed full of powerful bacteria that help to break down the leaves and get the nutrients out. A sloth's stomach can weigh as much as one third of its entire body!

THE ULTIMATE CAMOUFLAGE

As well as keeping still, sloths have another nifty trick that helps them blend into their leafy environment. Algae often grow on their fur, partly because they move so slowly, and the mottled green growth helps them look like just another plant.

COOL NAME, WHERE'D YOU GET IT?

The scientific name for **three-toed sloths** is Bradypodidae, meaning "slow of foot" in Ancient Greek. The name for **two-toed sloths** is Megalonychidae, also from Ancient Greek, and translates to "great claw."

STRONG ARMS AND SMALL LEGS

Sloths spend most of their time in trees—there's plenty of food up there, and it helps them stay safe from the predators who can't climb! But there's another reason sloths don't really hang out on the ground—they're not built for it. Sloth bodies aren't all that strong, and they have a lot less muscle than other animals of a similar size. The muscles they do have are cleverly arranged to be in the most useful places for climbing trees—the front of their bodies, especially in their arms. Their back legs are really weak by comparison, so when they do make a rare trip onto the ground, they rely on their front legs to do most of the work in dragging their bodies forward. Their huge claws make gripping onto branches easier, but unfortunately they get in the way when they're trying to walk on the ground. It's a lot like someone with really long fingernails trying to use a touch screen. **AWKWARD!**

THE SLOTH VERSION OF HEAD LICE

You're not the only one who thinks sloths are pretty cool. A particular kind of moth might just be their biggest fan. These moths make their home in the sloths' fur, where they can eat the algae growing on them and drink their sweat. If you think that's gross, wait until you hear about where they lay their eggs. These weird moths can't think of a better place for their babies to hatch than in a pile of sloth poo. What a way to enter the world!

SOLENODONS

Solenodons are particularly odd-looking, with bare, scaly tails a bit like an oversized rat's tail and feet that are almost comically large. They also grunt like pigs! Solenodons are extremely ancient (as in, lived-at-the-same-time-as-dinosaurs ancient) and highly endangered. They're one of only two native land mammals left in the Dominican Republic, and they've survived this long partly because they spend a lot of their time hidden away, and partly because they have a clever and very surprising way of protecting themselves.

ARE YOU SURE THAT'S MILK?

Solenodon mothers feed their babies with milk, but it doesn't come out near their tummies or chests like many other milk-producing animals. Instead, solenodons have nipples near their butts, in the fold where their back legs meet their bodies.

SMELL YOU LATER

Solenodons have a strong, musty smell that oozes out of special glands in their skin. They have been described as smelling like goats or wet dogs!

WHERE CAN I SEE A SOLENODON?

One species of solenodon lives in Haiti and the Dominican Republic, the other lives in Cuba.

RUN OR HIDE?

Solenodons can climb trees but spend most of their time low to the ground—sometimes even underneath it! During the day they hunker down in dens dug into the earth, or occasionally inside a cave or hollow log. They're pretty awkward animals, with a slow, shambling gait, although they can work up a decent speed if they're under threat. Even at their fastest they still aren't graceful—they run on their toes, swerving from side to side instead of moving in a straight line. Sometimes when they're afraid, they stop moving altogether and tuck their heads in, possibly hoping that if they can't see the predator, the predator can't see them.

SUPER SCARY SPIT

Solenodon means "groove-tooth" or "pipe-tooth" in Ancient Greek, and they earned their name because they have an extra-special feature. They're one of the only venomous mammals in the world, and the only kind that inject venom using their teeth! They have two sharp fangs, a bit like a snake. The venom is actually a very toxic saliva, and it flows through special grooves in the solenodon's fangs to reach its target. For smaller animals, the side effects can be severe. They include paralysis, convulsions, and difficulty breathing. The venom isn't able to kill a human, but swelling and quite a lot of pain will bother you for up to a week if you get bitten. So if you ever find yourself near a solenodon, avoid its teeth!

FANG PASTE

A NOSE FOR FOOD

- Solenodons are called "insectivores," because they mostly stick to eating insects. Every now and then they'll branch out and eat a frog or lizard, or roots, fruits, and other plant matter.

- Solenodons hunt at night, using the claws on their oversized feet to dig through the dirt and find food. They also use their claws to tear into rotting wood, gobbling up the insects that live inside.

- The eyes of a solenodon are small and beady—just like a chicken's. Their eyesight is pretty terrible, so they can't easily spot potential snacks.

- Luckily, solenodons have great hearing. They hunt using echolocation, like bats do. They make clicking sounds that bounce off objects around them, from trees and rocks to other animals, echoing back so the solenodons can learn where nearby prey is located.

- Solenodons have an excellent sense of smell. They use their upturned noses to root around in the earth and their long, sensitive whiskers to help them sense their prey. Their noses have a special joint in them that makes them extra flexible, a bit like how you have joints in your knees and elbows, so they're perfect for poking into hard-to-reach nooks and crannies.

TIGERS

Tigers live in China, India, Bangladesh, Cambodia, Thailand, Vietnam, Nepal, Malaysia, Bhutan, Myanmar, Laos, Indonesia, and Russia.

Not everyone has seen a tiger in person, but most people have seen plenty of pictures. They're big, they're stripy—what else is there to know? A lot! Including answers to pressing questions such as: What do tigers do with their leftovers? What does their pee smell like? And, most importantly, what does it mean when a tiger wags its tail?

JUST LIKE THE MOVIES

Many people are convinced that tiger pee smells just like a big, buttery bucket of popcorn.

A GROUP OF TiGERS CAN BE CALLED AN AMBUSH OR A STREAK.

CAN YOU OUTRUN A TIGER?

Tigers are a LOT faster than you. They can travel up to 40 miles per hour when they're in a serious hurry—easily as fast as a car.

HOW BIG IS A TIGER?

Tigers are the biggest felines in the entire world. **Siberian tigers** are the biggest of them all, weighing up to 800 pounds—about the same as five adult humans. They grow up to 11 feet long, and that's not even including their tail, which can sometimes extend nearly 3 feet on its own!

Sumatran tigers are the smallest, sometimes growing to less than half the length of their Siberian relatives. They are also considerably lighter, tipping the scale at a mere 300 pounds (mind you, that's still a lot more than you weigh!).

YOU CAN TELL A TIGER BY ITS STRIPES

Each individual tiger has a slightly different pattern of stripes—no two are the same, even if they're siblings. And they're not always orange with black stripes. They can be gold with pale orange stripes or white with pale tan stripes. And it's not just tigers' fur that's patterned—the skin below is just as stripy!

SHAVE CREAM

A YARD WITH A FENCE

Tigers mark their territory both with their scent and by scratching marks onto trees. They spread their scent by leaving puddles of pee and chunks of poo lying around—the stink of their urine can hang around for up to 40 days!

WHAT DOES A TIGER HAVE IN COMMON WITH A PET CAT?

When they're not using them, tigers can retract their claws back into their paws—a bit like a housecat. This helps keep their claws super sharp for when they need them—like when they're hooking into evasive prey.

39

FROM PRECIOUS BABY TO TERRIFYING BEAST

Tiger cubs can weigh less than 2 pounds at birth. At first, they're adorable little bundles of fluff that are completely reliant on their mothers for food and protection, but they mature quickly. By the time they're just one and a half years old, they're ready to start heading out to hunt.

WAGGING TAILS

A tiger's roar can travel an impressive distance—more than 1.9 miles! Tigers also use their long and expressive tails to communicate. But, unlike a pet dog, if a tiger is wagging its tail, it is NOT happy—it's often a sign of aggression. Even a twitching tail can be bad news—a relaxed tiger generally has an equally relaxed tail.

FAMILY TIES

Despite different appearances and habitats, the nearest living relatives to tigers are snow leopards. Tigers and lions are often lumped together, but they're actually not that closely related. It isn't just their stripes that set them apart—among other things, tiger brains are on average 16 percent bigger than lion brains! Tigers are extremely smart, learn quickly and have excellent memories.

ROOM TO SWING A CAT

Most tigers make their home in forested areas, where there is plenty of cover and lots of food to hunt. Tigers can climb trees but, despite often being surrounded by them, they generally prefer to keep their feet firmly on the ground.

Tigers usually like to live alone, and ideally their neighbors will live very far away—they're not the most sociable animals! **Siberian tigers** have huge territories—a single tiger can command more than 1,500 square miles. In places where real estate is more scarce, tigers are often forced to live much closer to each other—as many as 18 **Bengal tigers** can sometimes live in about 40 square miles.

ON THE HUNT

SPLISH SPLASH

Tigers often swim in rivers and lakes, and not just so they can hunt down animals in the water. They also like to splash around for fun, or to cool off when they get hot. They can swim up to 20 miles each day as they patrol their territory, and can easily swim across rivers that are 4 miles wide.

YOU CAN TELL JUST BY LOOKING AT A TIGER THAT THEY'RE PRETTY GOOD HUNTERS. THEIR HUGE TEETH AND SUPER-SHARP CLAWS KIND OF GIVE THEM AWAY . . .

▶ For animals of their size, tigers can be remarkably hard to spot. They're masters of stealth, relying on their striped coats to help them blend in with bars of shadow and light in their forest homes. They often slink low to the ground as they move, and their huge feet have plenty of padding to help them tread silently.

▶ Tigers usually hunt at night, and they're highly skilled at spotting even the tiniest movements of their prey. Their night vision is excellent—about six times better than yours.

▶ After stalking their target, they pounce and deliver a death blow, which for tigers is often a strong bite—usually around the neck area. Their teeth can be 3 inches long, and their jaws are powerful enough to snap the spines of their prey.

▶ Tigers usually hunt animals that are quite large, like deer, wild pigs, elk, antelope, and water buffalo. They also hunt animals that are pretty dangerous predators themselves, such as leopards, crocodiles, and pythons. They rarely eat humans, or even go near them.

▶ The average tiger meal weighs about 11 pounds, but tigers can eat up to 60 pounds of food in a single night. The animals they kill are often much larger than that, so what do they do with the leftovers? They don't have a fridge to pop them in, so they do the next best thing—cover the half-eaten corpse with leaves, so they can come back to it later.

▶ Sometimes tigers share their food. Once, an **Indian tiger** killed a large antelope and eight of her relatives came to visit over the next day or so to get involved in the feast.

41

WOLVES

The clichéd image of a lone wolf with its head thrown back, howling at the moon, is one that most people are familiar with. But wolves are far more fascinating than that—they are remarkably hardy creatures, and can have particularly odd habits, such as running marathons or taking long ocean swims.

SHADES OF GRAY

Gray wolves aren't always gray—they can be black, white, or any shade of gray between the two.

Wolves are one of the most widespread animals in the world. **Gray wolves** live all over the western hemisphere, from Arctic wolves in Greenland and parts of North America to sea wolves off the coast of Canada. **Red wolves** only live in one area of North Carolina, a refuge on the Albemarle Peninsula.

A GROUP OF WOLVES IS CALLED A PACK. EVEN A SINGLE PAIR OF WOLVES CAN BE CALLED A PACK AS LONG AS THEY HAVE THEIR OWN TERRITORY.

TOP DOG
PARENTS

Wolves almost always live in groups, generally led by a dominant pair. These top dogs are called the "alpha male" and "alpha female." There are usually between six and ten wolves in a pack, and many of them are the grown-up pups of the alphas (that never left home!).

▶ The alpha pair are often the only wolves in the pack that have babies, but the other wolves are all involved in raising the pups. Pups can't see or hear for the first few weeks, so having a whole pack to look out for them helps keep them out of trouble!

▶ Milk is the first thing pups consume, then they move on to food that has been chewed up and spat back out by older wolves, until they're finally old enough to tackle solid food.

▶ Wolf pups are very playful and love to wrestle and leap around. Sometimes they even play tag or tug of war—games that help prepare them for hunting as an adult wolf.

▶ Baby wolves can't go to the toilet by themselves—their mother needs to lick them to help their bodily waste come out.

FLANNERY FILE

I've slept next to a wolf. I've fed a wolf. I've walked alongside a wolf. He was my best friend, and his name was Butch. It's not quite what you're thinking, though . . . Butch was my dog—a black labrador. Dogs are really just specialized wolf breeds. Wolves' scientific name, *Canis*, even means "dog" in Latin! I was 7 when I got Butch, and I had him for 15 years. He was a really big part of my life, and such a sweetheart—we shared every adventure together.

REAL OR MYTH?

Dire wolves were native North American wolves that preyed on the now extinct American megafauna. These wolves became extinct around 9,500 years ago, when their giant walking meals also died out—it's hard to thrive when there's nothing good to eat. They were really big, but the largest **gray wolves** living today are actually similar in size. After dire wolves disappeared, gray wolves came in from Asia and Alaska and filled the space their extinction had left.

43

OFF THE BEATEN TRACK

WOLVES LIVE IN A WHOLE LOT OF DIFFERENT HABITATS, BUT THEY USUALLY PREFER TO MAKE THEIR HOMES IN PLACES THAT ARE QUITE REMOTE.

▶ Wolves can live at temperatures as low as −40 degrees Fahrenheit and as high as 122 degrees Fahrenheit!

▶ Some types of **gray wolf** live near the beach and are surprisingly good swimmers! They are sometimes called "sea wolves," "rain wolves," or "beachcombing wolves." They live around the coast of British Columbia, often swimming over 7 miles through cold, choppy water to reach islands off the coast. Their diet reflects their closeness to the ocean and includes things like shellfish, crabs, clams, fish, barnacles, fish eggs, seals, and even dead whales that wash up onto the beach.

▶ Many wolves choose to live in wooded areas—trees make it easier to stay out of sight, and food is often more plentiful. Forests also have lots of good places to make dens for their pups, from hollow trees to dens dug into the dirt.

▶ Arctic wolves live in cold, unforgiving climates—places where ice and frozen ground mean they can't dig dens. They live in caves or rock crevices instead, relying on their extra layer of fur to stay warm in sub-zero temperatures. In some wolf habitats it can be dark for five months of the year! When spring finally arrives, bringing light and warmth, the wolves shed their underlayer of fur so they don't overheat, kind of like taking off your sweater so you're just wearing a coat.

CLIMATE CHANGE

The **Ethiopian wolf**'s habitat in the mountains of Ethiopia is shrinking due to climate change, and the Arctic wolf is also under threat—its icy habitat is becoming warmer and food is getting harder to find.

HAVING A
HOWL

- Just as you talk to your family, wolves communicate with other wolves in the pack—by howling.

  - Wolves often howl as a way of marking their territory—if a whole pack is howling in unison, it might be to let nearby wolves know they're on someone else's turf . . . so back off!

- Sometimes howls are a warning sign that a wolf is ready to attack, but not always—sometimes a wolf just howls because it hears another wolf howling, a bit like you might yawn if you see someone near you yawning.

- Howls can travel extraordinary distances—up to 6 miles—so just because you can hear a wolf doesn't mean it's particularly close.

PAW PATROL

Wolves can have huge paws—the average wolf pawprint can be as big as a sandwich!

ON THE HUNT

- Wolves are carnivores and skilled hunters, often going after prey much larger than them such as elk, deer, moose, and caribou. The musk ox, which is eaten by Arctic wolves, can weigh ten times as much as the wolf hunting it!

- Wolves can eat up to 22 pounds of food in one go! Hunting large animals isn't easy, so when wolves make a kill, they don't let any of the meal go to waste—even if that means eating until they're ready to burst. Sometimes they don't eat for a week or more, so they really appreciate their meals when they can get them.

- Wolves won't turn their noses up at much—fish, birds, lizards, and snakes are all acceptable snacks. Meat is their main food source, but it's not unheard of for wolves to munch on fruit, such as berries, from time to time.

- Wolves often chase prey for a long time to tire it out so it's easier to kill. Sometimes they cover more than 12 miles in one go!

- Wolves often hunt as a group, using teamwork to bring down their prey. Hunting as a team means eating as a group, but not everyone gets an equal share—the dominant pair of wolves in the pack get to eat before everyone else, often snagging the best parts.

PRIMATES

Primates are a group of animals that includes monkeys, apes, lemurs, tarsiers, and . . . **YOU!** Yes, you're related to all of those animals—which explains why some of the things they do seem oddly human. Have you ever seen an ape holding hands with a friend, cuddling a baby, or flashing a big toothy smile? The resemblance can be uncanny. But despite the similarities, there are plenty of differences between you and your primate relatives. For example, would you eat a bug you'd just picked out of your friend's hair?

GOTTA FIND 'EM ALL

New species of primates are still being discovered around the world. Most of the new species are smaller primates, such as **lemurs** and **bushbabies**. But a new species of **orangutan** from Sumatra was named as recently as 2017!

WHERE CAN I SEE A PRIMATE?

Various types of monkeys live in Africa, Asia, and South America, and just one kind lives in Europe—the **Barbary macaque**, which lives in Gibraltar.

Great apes (aside from humans) live in countries across Asia and Africa, while lesser apes are only found in Asia.

Lemurs only live in Madagascar, plus on a few very small islands nearby.

WHO'S WHO?

Primates are a pretty big group, so it can be tricky to keep them straight. They're loosely divided into two groups—the **lemurs**, **lorises**, and **aye-ayes** sit in a group called the Strepsirrhini and the **monkeys**, **apes**, and **tarsiers** sit in a group called the Haplorhini. You fit into the second group, too.

▶ Although **gorillas**, **chimpanzees**, and **orangutans** are often called monkeys, they're actually all types of ape. So how do you tell the difference between apes and monkeys? Well, apes don't have tails, are able to walk on two legs, and are even smarter than monkeys (who are already pretty clever!). They're also usually bigger. There are two groups of apes—great apes and lesser apes. Great apes include **gorillas**, **orangutans**, **chimpanzees**, and **bonobos**. Lesser apes include **gibbons** and **siamangs**.

▶ There are heaps of kinds of monkeys, too! They're split into two broad groups: Old World and New World. Old World monkeys live in Asia and Africa, while New World monkeys live across South and North America. Old World monkeys can live on the ground or in trees, and they have special leathery patches of skin on their butts that make sitting on the ground more comfortable. New World monkeys always live in trees, and their flexible tails can be used to grasp tree branches—they're almost like an extra arm! Old World monkeys often have longer noses with small, close-together nostrils that usually face downward like yours, whereas New World monkeys have shorter noses with nostrils set further apart and facing more toward the sides.

▶ **Tarsiers** started to evolve in a separate direction from apes and monkeys way back when dinosaurs were becoming extinct, which is why they look quite different.

WHAT BIG TEETH YOU HAVE!

When a monkey smiles at you, it doesn't mean they want to be friends. It's actually a warning sign that means the monkey is feeling threatened.

KEEPING CLEAN

Primates often bond by grooming each other—brushing and stroking each other's fur and picking bugs out, too. Sometimes they even eat the bugs—and yet, they have quite strict hygiene standards. For example, **mandrills** avoid grooming monkeys that are infected with parasites. How do they recognize which monkeys are infected? By smelling their poop, of course! Because they stop grooming the infected monkeys until they're better, they stop the parasites from spreading.

CLEVER!

AND THE WINNER IS ...

The award for the weirdest-looking primate has to go to the **aye-ayes**! They have long, white hairs sprinkled over their darker fur that they can puff out to make themselves look bigger, plus outlandishly large ears. Their sharp incisor teeth keep on growing over time, kind of like fingernails do. And, speaking of fingers, aye-ayes have a totally bizarre middle finger that is longer than the others and looks like it is made purely of bone with just a thin coating of skin stretched over it. These weird digits are extra-sensitive, so they're what aye-ayes use to feel their way around.

WHAT DOES A MONKEY LOOK LIKE?

COOL!

If you think the different hairstyles humans have come up with are impressive, just wait until you get a good look at what other primates are sporting.

▶ **Golden lion tamarins** have small black faces surrounded by a thick, mane-like fringe of glossy orange fur.

▶ Mature male gorillas are sometimes called "silverbacks" because of the large patch of silvery fur on their backs.

▶ **Bonobo** hair is quite long, and it often parts naturally in the center of their heads and fluffs out around their ears in a style that looks oddly human.

▶ **Ring-tailed lemurs** are mostly gray or brown with cream underbellies, but their long, bushy tails are covered in black-and-white rings.

▶ **Golden snub-nosed monkeys** have thick orange fur and

BIGGEST AND SMALLEST

Great apes are the largest of all the primates, and **mountain gorillas** are the ultimate giants. They can be close to 6 feet tall and weigh about 485 pounds. **Orangutans** are smaller, under 5 feet and more like 440 pounds, but they deserve a special mention for being the biggest mammals to live in trees!

When it comes to monkeys, **mandrills** are the largest. They can grow up to 3 feet tall, which is the average height of a four-year-old child. Their weight is closer to a ten-year-old child, though—they can weigh more than 75 pounds.

The smallest monkey is the **pygmy marmoset**, which isn't quite 5 inches tall and only weighs about 3 ounces—about the same as a deck of cards.

If you think that's small, wait until you hear about **lemurs**. Although some of them can be quite large, **mouse lemurs** can be well under 2 inches tall and weigh less than 1 ounce.

bare blue faces. Their noses are so reduced that they look a bit like the nose cavities on human skulls.

▶ **Blue-eyed black lemurs** aren't all black—only the males are, with females having fur in shades of brown. Blue-eyed black lemurs are also the only primates other than humans that have blue eyes.

▶ **Emperor tamarins** have very long white mustaches that droop down on either side of their mouths. It's not just the male monkeys that sport these impressive 'staches—female monkeys grow them, too!

▶ **White-faced sakis** are very large, stocky monkeys. They grow black fur all over, except for a section of white fur

that puffs up all across their faces—only their eyes and noses poke through.

▶ **De Brazza's monkeys** have long white goatees and distinctive furry brown foreheads. The black fur on their heads is so neatly shaped that it looks like they've just been to the barber.

STRANGE EATING HABITS

PRIMATES HAVE SOME BIZARRE FOOD PREFERENCES—THERE'S NO ACCOUNTING FOR TASTE.

WHAT IS A GROUP OF PRIMATES CALLED?

A group of **monkeys** or **lemurs** is called a troop, and **gorillas** can be either a troop or a band (not the kind with instruments). A group of **chimpanzees** is sometimes called a community, and a group of **apes** is often referred to as a tribe, or sometimes a shrewdness.

▶ **Proboscis monkeys** only eat unripe fruit. Ripe fruit is packed with sugar, and as the sugar breaks down in the monkeys' stomachs it can make them swell up and even kill them.

▶ Male **gorillas** can eat 40 pounds of food each day. They mostly eat green, leafy plants.

▶ Many lemurs, including **red ruffed lemurs** and **mongoose lemurs**, love to eat nectar from flowers. They stick their noses deep inside to reach it, getting their snouts covered in pollen in the process. Mongoose lemurs also eat the flowers themselves!

▶ Some **red colobus monkeys** eat charcoal from burned trees, but not because they think it's delicious—it's thought that the charcoal helps get rid of the toxins that they eat when they munch on certain types of leaves.

▶ Up to 90 percent of a **bamboo lemur's** diet can consist of bamboo. Different species of bamboo lemur eat different parts of the bamboo, which means they don't have to fight over their food as much. Some prefer the young, tender shoots, others love the soft core of the bamboo stalk, which they have to shred their way through to.

▶ Some **macaque monkeys** living in Japan wash their food, such as potatoes, before eating it. Sometimes they use fresh water, but when they wash in salt water, they often dip their potatoes back in after each bite. Maybe they've realized salt and potato are the perfect flavor combination!

HUNTING AND FORAGING

▶ **Tarsiers** are excellent hunters. They can go after insects, birds, and even snakes! They are silent but deadly, leaping down onto their prey and using their sharp teeth to kill it.

▶ **Aye-ayes** tap on branches with their long middle finger to find the hollow insect tunnels under the bark. Once they find one, they use the same finger to tear into the wood and pull out the insects and larvae inside.

▶ "Don't poop where you eat" is a common saying, but **mouse lemurs** do exactly that! They poo near their homes and the seeds of the fruits they've gobbled down sprout into new plants, helped by the rich compost of the poo. The lemurs are eventually surrounded by the exact plants they like to eat, right outside their home. **CONVENIENT!**

ARE ALL TAILS EQUAL?

Lemurs have long, bendy tails that look like they would be perfect for clinging to branches or swinging through the trees. But they're not! Unlike those of New World monkeys, lemur tails can't grasp onto things—they're really only useful for balance.

FLANNERY FILE

I had a terrifying interaction with a **gorilla** once. I was visiting a zoo in the United States and was taken behind the scenes to the area where the zookeepers fed the animals. I was walking along a corridor behind the gorilla enclosure when I suddenly felt an enormous rumbling. I thought there was an earthquake! Everything started shaking, and there was a deafening roaring noise. I turned around and came face to face with an adult male gorilla by the name of Caesar—he had thrown himself at the wire mesh fence and was staring straight at me. I felt my pulse speed up as my body went into fight or flight. This intimidating animal—who weighed over 400 pounds—was stomping, roaring, and baring his teeth at me, and there was just a wire mesh fence between us!

A TRUSTY TOOLBOX

PRIMATES OFTEN USE THEIR HANDS AND TEETH TO CRACK OPEN FRUITS, SEEDS, AND NUTS, BUT SOMETIMES THEY'RE JUST NOT STRONG ENOUGH TO DO IT ALONE—SO SOME OF THEM HAVE LEARNED TO USE TOOLS!

▶ **Capuchins** smash open cashews by placing them on a rock and hitting them with another rock to reach the tasty nut inside. Stone tools can also be used to crack open fruit seed kernels and even different types of shellfish, like crabs. These monkeys use sticks to dig up things like roots and lizard eggs, or to fish hard-to-reach snacks out of narrow spaces, such as rock crevices.

▶ **Chimpanzees** mostly eat fruit, but will also eat insects, eggs, and even animals such as monkeys or wild pigs. They often use rocks to crack open the husks and shells of plants or animals, plus they poke sticks into ant and termite nests to scoop out the critters inside, spooning them straight into their mouths. They can also use leaves to scoop up water to drink!

CREATURE FEATURES

Not all primates have the same kinds of features—and some are a lot bigger than others.

- **Spider monkeys** have long, lanky arms and incredibly flexible tails. Their tails can grow to nearly 3 feet long, which far outstrips the length of their bodies.

- **Tarsiers** have HUGE eyes—each one is as big as their entire brain. For some species, such as the **Philippine tarsier**, each eye is bigger than their stomach.

- Male **proboscis monkeys** have simply enormous noses. The larger the nose, the more likely they are to attract mates. Their noses aren't just decorative—they can also be used to make loud honking sounds to assert dominance.

- **Orangutans** have ridiculously long arms that nearly reach the ground even when standing upright. Their arm span can be over 6 feet!

- Some **lemurs** store excess fat in their tails and back legs, so they can survive without food in times of rest. Sometimes, 40 percent of a **fat-tailed dwarf lemur's** body weight is packed into its tail.

FLANNERY FILE

I've had some really heartwarming experiences with primates. Once I went to the zoo with my wife and brand-new baby, and we were sitting outside the **chimpanzee** enclosure. Chimpanzees often interact with people quite a bit, but they also get bored and wander off if the people aren't doing anything interesting. This was a quiet morning at the zoo—no one was really around—so the chimpanzees were off doing their own thing. But when my wife started breastfeeding our little baby, every female chimpanzee in the enclosure stopped what they were doing and looked at her. They came over to the window and watched and watched. It was like they were thinking, *They do that as well?* It was incredible. They were completely mesmerized! Chimps are very chatty, but as soon as this happened, they started talking in a different tone—it seemed like they were saying, "Come over and look at this. It's amazing!"

MONKEY CHATS

Just like humans, groups of primates often like to chat. They communicate about all sorts of things, telling each other when they've found food, marking their territory, attracting mates or spreading the word that a predator is approaching. Not all of the ways they communicate are verbal— sometimes they use body language and gestures, but chattering is very common.

▶ **Bonobos** have one of the broadest ranges of sounds of all the apes, with about 40 different calls that include grunts, yells, squeals, growls, and screams, plus a particular squeaking sound that appears to mean different things depending on what the ape is doing when they make it.

▶ **Ring-tailed lemurs** use lots of vocal calls, but also use visual cues to stay in touch. They often hold their striking tails up in the air as they travel so it is easier for the group to see which way everyone is moving and stay together.

▶ **Chimpanzees** make a whole range of sounds, from hoots and yells to grunts. Sometimes they even laugh as they play together, including when they're being tickled! They also have very expressive faces, which they use to communicate, plus a whole lot of hand gestures.

▶ **Diana monkeys** have one of the most sophisticated monkey languages. They don't just have one alarm call, they have a different sound for each predator! They also combine different individual calls to say longer, more complex things—kind of like how you string words together to form sentences. Not only is their own language quite detailed, but they can actually understand the calls of other monkey species living nearby. They're fluent in multiple monkey languages!

▶ **Mountain gorillas** show their dominance using vocal calls such as hoots and roars, plus plenty of body language. They are often seen beating their chest or standing up on their back legs to appear tall and threatening.

▶ **Howler monkeys** have the loudest voices of any monkey. Groups of them often call all at once to mark their territory, and they're so loud that they can be heard nearly 3 miles away.

JUST ADD WATER

GIRLS RUN THE WORLD

Some primate species are dominated by males, but plenty of them go the other way. **Bonobos**, who are led by females, have some of the most peaceful communities of all the primates. They're good at sharing and usually coexist very happily. Most lemur species, including **ring-tailed lemurs** and **mouse lemurs**, also have dominant females. While males move from group to group, females will stay with the same group for their entire lives.

▶ **Japanese macaques** take outdoor baths in winter to stay warm. It gets very snowy where they live, so taking a nice long soak in a hot spring helps ward off the winter chill. Even though they like to stay warm, they still enjoy the snow—they actually like to play in it, sometimes even rolling up snowballs just like humans do.

▶ **Proboscis monkeys** are particularly good swimmers and can even leap down into the water from the trees. They have special webbing on their feet and hands to help them swim better, kind of like built-in flippers!

▶ Sometimes the last thing **chimpanzees** and **orangutans** want is to get wet, so they use large leaves as umbrellas, holding them over their heads to keep the rain off.

54

CLIMATE CHANGE

Deforestation is a big issue for primates, as they're losing many of the places they can live in. This is a particular issue for animals that have highly specific habitats, such as **lemurs** on the island of Madagascar. Some primates are found only in cool habitats on mountain summits. As the earth warms, they will be pushed ever higher, until there isn't anywhere else to go that will suit them.

Lots of primates help plants to grow and spread, because they eat their fruits and then poop them out in a handy pile of dung that helps the plants to sprout and grow. Unfortunately, even with all their eating and pooping they're no match for how fast humans are cutting trees down in some areas.

> **Bushbabies** mark their territory using urine, but instead of peeing straight onto branches, they pee *into* their hands and then rub it on the trees.

BEGONE, PEST!

A range of monkeys, including **capuchins** and **spider monkeys**, have been known to rub crushed insects and the leaves of certain plants on their bodies. It seems they do this to deter insects from biting them—they do it more often when there are extra insects around.

Tamarin monkeys also use parts of plants to ward off pests—it is thought that they swallow large seeds to push out parasites that are living inside their bodies.

TAKING CARE OF A BABY

- Baby primates often just look like cuter, smaller versions of their parents, but not **François' langur monkeys**. As adults, they have silky black fur with two striking patches of white on their cheeks, but as babies they're bright orange all over! Their fur eventually changes to black as they mature.

- **Apes** often take care of their babies for much longer than many other animals—until they're at least seven years old, but sometimes into their teenage years.

- Lots of primates find new mates regularly, but not **gibbons**—they stick with their partner long-term, generally living together with their children.

- Baby **lemurs**, called "pups," are carried in their parents' mouths when they're really small. Once they get a little older they like to hitch rides by clinging to their mother's tummy or sitting up on her back—as if they're riding a motorcycle. Sometimes parents get grouchy, especially when the pups are old enough to walk, so they gently bite them until they get off!

- Some **lorises** and **lemurs** don't carry their babies around as they set off looking for food. Instead, they find a cozy place to leave them near where they're foraging, then come back to pick them up before heading home. It's a bit like dropping a kid at daycare before heading to work, only there are no adults in charge—the babies are usually left alone! This tactic works fine when the babies are too small to move by themselves, but once they get older they can sometimes wander off and need to be tracked down.

GLOSSARY

ALGAE

Algae are a large and wide-ranging group of organisms, most of which are aquatic. Some are microscopic, while others (like many types of seaweed) can grow to be very large. They can be found in both salt water and fresh water.

ALPHA MALE/FEMALE

The alpha is the most powerful individual in a group of animals—the leader. There can be alpha males or alpha females, and some groups of animals are led by a pair of alphas—both male and female. Alphas usually gain leadership by fighting and defeating the former alpha.

AQUATIC

Aquatic animals are those that spend all or most of their time in the water.

ARBOREAL

Arboreal animals are those that spend all or most of their time in trees.

ATMOSPHERE

Atmosphere is the gases surrounding a planet, held there by the planet's gravity. Earth's atmosphere is a very thin layer of air between the earth's surface and the edge of space.

ATROPHY

Atrophy is the wasting away or degeneration of a part of the body. It can happen for many reasons, including the body part no longer being used or a lack of nutrition.

BACTERIA

Bacteria are microscopic single-celled organisms. They can be found in many different places: in the soil, air, and water, as well as on and inside plants and animals—including humans. Some bacteria are beneficial to us, whereas others are destructive.

CANINE

A canine is an animal belonging to the Canidae family, or dog family. This includes wolves, jackals, hyenas, coyotes, foxes, dingoes, and domestic dogs.

CARBON

Carbon is a chemical element. It is one of the building blocks that plants and animals are made from, making it essential to all life on Earth. All organic compounds are considered "carbon-based." Carbon can combine with other elements to make new compounds.

CARBON DIOXIDE

Carbon dioxide is a compound made up of one carbon atom (C) and two oxygen atoms (O_2). It is a greenhouse gas, which means it traps the sun's heat close to the earth instead of allowing it to move out into space. Too much carbon dioxide causes the earth to overheat and, as the weather changes, many plants and animals are negatively affected. This is called global warming, or climate change.

CARBON EMISSIONS

When we burn carbon-rich fossil fuels, we release a huge amount of carbon into the air. The carbon then bonds with oxygen to produce carbon dioxide. Over time, the amount of carbon in the atmosphere has risen drastically due to the increased use of fossil fuels.

CARNIVORE/ CARNIVOROUS

Carnivores are animals that exclusively or primarily eat meat—either by killing their meal or by scavenging carcasses.

COLD-BLOODED AND WARM-BLOODED ANIMALS

Warm-blooded animals, or endotherms, use their metabolism to generate the right amount of heat to keep their bodies at the right temperature. Cold-blooded animals, or ectotherms, aren't able to control their body temperature using their metabolism. On cold days, their metabolism drops along with their body temperature, which slows down their physical movement. Endotherms generally need a steady food supply to keep their metabolism generating heat, while ectotherms can often survive long periods without food, thanks to their ability to slow their bodies down and wait out the colder months.

CONTINENTS

A continent is a large landmass, and one continent often includes multiple countries. The continents of the world are Europe, Asia, Africa, North and South America, Australia, and Antarctica.

DEFORESTATION

Deforestation is the permanent destruction of forests. People clear the land to graze farmed animals such as cattle, as well as to build or to harvest wood any other tree products (such as palm oil). Deforestation causes habitat loss for many animals and can lead to the extinction of species that need the forest to survive. It also reduces the number of trees taking CO_2 out of the atmosphere, which means that our atmosphere fills up with more greenhouse gas emissions.

DOMESTICATED SPECIES

Domesticated species are animals that have been bred to benefit humans, often over many generations. Animals are often domesticated so that humans can use parts of their bodies (such as flesh, skin, fur, or bone), or things that they produce (such as milk or eggs), for food, clothing, and decoration. Animals are also often domesticated to use as labor or to keep as pets.

ECHOLOCATION

Echolocation is the use of echoes and soundwaves to find out where an object is in space. Many animals use echolocation to hunt and navigate, like dolphins, whales, bats, and some bird species.

ECOSYSTEM

An ecosystem is a finely balanced environment, in which all the living things (plants, animals and other organisms) and nonliving things (like rocks and the weather) work together to maintain the system's health.

FELINE

Felines are members of the Felidae (or cat) family. They are all carnivorous mammals. Felines include lions, tigers, and domestic cats.

FERAL ANIMALS

Feral animals are domesticated animals that have been released into the wild and continued to reproduce there—for example, feral cats, goats, camels, and dogs. Feral animals can often endanger the lives of wild animals by preying on them.

FORAGING

When an animal searches for food in the wild, this is called foraging.

FOSSIL FUELS

Fossil fuels are made from fossilized plants and animals that have been buried under the soil for millions of years. Fossil fuels include things like oil, coal, and natural gas.

GREENHOUSE GAS EMISSIONS

Greenhouse gases absorb the heat that radiates off the earth's surface and bounce it back, trapping heat in the atmosphere rather than releasing it into space. The main greenhouse gases are water vapor, carbon dioxide, methane, and nitrous oxide. Fossil fuels are the biggest human cause of greenhouse gas emissions.

HERBIVORE/ HERBIVOROUS

Herbivores are animals that have an exclusively or primarily plant-based diet.

HIBERNATION

Hibernation is a type of deep rest that some endotherms, or warm-blooded animals, go into. Hibernation often occurs when animals don't have access to enough food or when it's too cold—certain species of animal hibernate over winter every year. During hibernation, body temperatures drop and metabolisms slow down as animals become inactive.

HIERARCHY

Hierarchy refers to a power structure within a group of animals. An alpha or an alpha pair is generally at the top of the hierarchy, with other members of the group having varying degrees of power below them. Omegas are the least powerful members of the hierarchy.

HORMONES

Hormones are chemicals inside plants and animals that help all of these living things to function. In plants, hormones help to control growth, as well as the production of flowers or fruit. In animals, hormones are used to send messages to different parts of the body to help it operate. Hormones affect all sorts of things, like growth, sleep, temperature, hunger, and much more.

HUNTING

For animals, hunting is the activity of killing and eating other animals. For humans, hunting also includes killing animals, but not always for food.

HYPERPHAGIA

Hyperphagia is a hugely increased appetite, and usually prompts eating a lot more than usual. Many animals go into hyperphagia to prepare themselves for hibernation (a period in which they don't eat at all).

INCUBATION

Incubation is the process of keeping eggs at the right temperature while embryos grow inside them. Different animals incubate their eggs in different ways, such as sitting on them or burying them in sand, dirt, or plant matter.

INVERTEBRATE

Invertebrates lack a backbone; they either have a gooey, spongy body (like jellyfish and worms) or they have an exoskeleton (like insects and crabs).

LARVAE

Many animals begin their life as larvae before eventually growing into their adult form. Larvae generally look completely different from their parents, and often need very different conditions to survive. For example, tadpoles are the larvae of frogs, and caterpillars are the larvae of butterflies.

MAMMALS

Mammals are a very broad class of animals. Some walk, some swim, and some fly, and their diets can vary from carnivorous to herbivorous, but they all have a number of traits in common, including that they have hair or fur, feed their young with milk, and are warm-blooded.

MARSUPIALS

Marsupials are a group of mammals. Most female marsupials have a pouch where they keep their babies when they're very young, so that they can continue to grow and develop in a safe, warm place. Some marsupial species are herbivores, others are carnivores, and there are also some omnivorous species. Most of the world's marsupials live in Australia and South America.

MEGAFAUNA

The word "megafauna" means "giant animal." It is most commonly used to refer to animals from the Pleistocene epoch (the end of the last ice age), which are the larger ancestors of animals alive today. However, species that are alive today can also be referred to as megafauna —common examples include elephants, rhinos, hippos, giraffes, lions, bears, and whales.

METABOLISM

Metabolism refers to the chemical reactions that happen inside an organism to keep it alive. There are many different metabolic reactions, but the main ones involve releasing energy or using energy. For example, an animal's metabolism digests the food it eats and converts that food into a form that can be released as energy. Animals also use their energy to grow and repair their bodies.

NOCTURNAL

Nocturnal animals are active during the night and rest during the day.

OMNIVORE/OMNIVOROUS

Omnivores are animals that eat a variety of meat and plant matter.

ORGANISM

An organism is an animal, a plant or a single-celled life form.

OXYGEN

Oxygen is a gas that makes up part of the air we breathe. It's highly reactive, which means it bonds easily with other elements (for example, carbon). Animals rely on oxygen to survive—they breathe it in and use it to convert nutrients into energy, releasing carbon dioxide as a waste product of this process. Plants exist in perfect symbiosis with animals, as they absorb carbon dioxide and release oxygen.

PARASITE

A parasite is an organism that makes its home in or on an organism of another species, relying on it for food, shelter, and everything else it needs to live. The organism that a parasite makes its home on is called its "host."

PHEROMONES

Pheromones are a type of hormone—a chemical that some animals release to communicate with other members of their species. Pheromones can be released for many reasons, including to attract a mate, to mark pathways leading to home or food, and even as a warning sign.

PIGMENT

Pigments are colored chemicals in the tissues of animals. Some animals produce their own pigments, whereas others get them from their food.

POLLINATION

Pollination is the way that plants reproduce to create seeds and fruits. Pollination involves the movement of pollen from the male part of a flower (the anther) to the female part (the stigma). Some plants self-pollinate, meaning that the transfer of pollen happens within a single flower, or between different flowers on the same plant. The other form of pollination is cross-pollination, where pollen travels between different plants. Things like wind and water can help pollen to travel between plants, but many plants rely on "pollinators"—animals such as birds and insects—to transfer their pollen.

POLLUTION

Pollution is the introduction of harmful materials or substances into our environment. The three main types of pollution are water, air, and land pollution. Some examples of pollutants are microplastics in the ocean, greenhouse gas emissions in the atmosphere, and pesticides used in agriculture.

PREDATOR

In zoology, "predator" usually refers to an animal that hunts other animals for food. Parasites are also a kind of predator. Predators are essential to a balanced ecosystem.

PREHENSILE

A prehensile body part is one that can grab on to things. Many different body parts can be prehensile, including tails, noses, hands, and feet.

PROBOSCIS

A proboscis is a long, flexible snout or feeding organ. Many insects use a proboscis to eat, like some moths and butterflies, but larger animal species can also have a proboscis—like elephants and solenodons.

TERRESTRIAL

Terrestrial animals are those that spend all or most of their time on land.

TERRITORY

An animal's territory is the area of land or water that it lives in, claims as its own and defends against trespassers.

TIDE

The tide is the periodic rise and fall of the ocean. Changes in the tide are caused by the earth spinning around, and by the gravitational pull of the sun and the moon.

VERTEBRATE

Vertebrates are animals that have a spine and a well-developed skeleton inside their bodies.

INDEX

ACKNOWLEDGMENTS

I'd like to thank Jane Novak for suggesting this project to me, and the fantastic team at Hardie Grant Egmont, especially Ella Meave. Without their dedication, this book would never have seen the light of day. I'd also like to thank Sam Caldwell for his brilliant illustrations, and Pooja Desai and Kristy Lund-White for their magnificent design work. I owe much gratitude to my wife Kate Holden and our son Coleby. They put up with long absences as I wrote this book. Many colleagues helped me with information, among whom Kris Helgen and Luigi Boitani deserve special mention.